FROM THE WOMB
TO THE PLANTATION
TO THE
PENITENTIARY

FROM THE WOMB TO THE PLANTATION TO THE PENITENTIARY

MARION LAMAR REED SR.

Kravitz & Sons
INNOVATORS IN PUBLISHING, MARKETING AND ADVERTISING

Kravitz and Sons LLC
1301 Farmville Blvd, Suite 104
Greenville, NC 27834

Published by Kravitz and Sons LLC.

ISBN: 979-8-89639-208-8 (sc)
ISBN: 979-8-89639-209-5 (e)

Library of Congress Control Number: 2025904529

TABLE OF CONTENTS

CHAPTER 1
    The Birth of the Black and Brown Man in Society 1

CHAPTER 2
    The Level of Education 11

CHAPTER 3
    Inside a Jail Cell Unit 18

CHAPTER 4
    The Black Church 27

CHAPTER 5
    The Plight of the Community 34

SUMMATION 39

ABOUT THE AUTHOR 43

In this book, I will try to convey the struggles of Black and Brown men in our society and what has changed their lives in the past fifty years. Since the civil rights movement back in 1954, I can remember that Black and Brown men were fighting for equality. Now there were women also involved in the movement as well to uphold the same cause for equal rights in America. Back in 1954, there were struggles for equality in education, the right to vote, and equal employment for Black and Brown men in America. Born from the womb freely, the cultural structure of these minority men was still on the planation. They could never be equal to their White counterparts. But the concept of freedom is totally different in America for the minority of Black and Brown men. Some of the White counterparts divided the family and sell off the family members so they could not ever get back together again. Black and Brown men and women were sold off just like cattle and horses were sold off for profit to slave owners.

In the plantation, the social atmosphere was separated by a caste system. History has it that the house nigger and the field nigger always worked just to survive on the plantation. This started the first caste system in the Black race in America. The lighter you were, you worked in the master's house. The darker you were, you worked in the cotton, potatoes, tobacco, and any other fields that were being planted. The women on the plantations were selected by the master to sleep with, and they were usually the house niggers. When a child was born out of that relationship, the child was called a mulatto. This created division between the Black race. This is one of the reasons the Black race has a caste system in society today. This system even carried over to levels of education, employment, and the type of housing for the Black and Brown men in America.

Now, slavery has somewhat changed because there are some dealings with institutionalized slavery; there is really no more plantation mindset. However, there are still some White Americans who will not release the beliefs of total freedom and equality for Black and Brown men in the twenty-first century simply because some of the Black and Brown men refuse to grow up and change their behaviors toward society. Some Black and Brown men believe that America still owes them some type of payback for many years of slavery.

In many cities across America, the drug scene has been a type of genocide for the Black and Brown men and women as well. The war on drugs back in 1982, when then President Ronald Reagan was in the White House, created havoc for the neighborhoods of Black and Brown men. The words "who let the dogs out" in certain neighborhoods also helped with racial profiling among many people of color in the urban as well as suburban areas. There is constant police pressure in the hood to degrade the Black and Brown men of their freedom and dignity.

In America today, in the south, they are still burning some churches, particularly in Alabama and Tennessee. The FBI and the ATF are agencies looking into this matter. They seem to be still looking. The church in Charlotte, North Carolina, where people were having a Bible study were gunned down. The critical aspect of gun control in our society has created an open-up-and-shoot-them-now-before-they-run. This was a record back in the sixties called "Shotgun" by JR Walker & The All Stars—shoot him before he runs now. In the twenty-first century, where are we now as a people in United States? Black and Brown men are born of the womb in a society, and the progress as a whole still suffers for equality and respect.

In 2015, this was President Barak Obama's last stand as president of the United States of America, and if Black and Brown men don't get the message by now, when will they get it? Nigger, wake up. Nigger, get a job. Nigger, pull your pants up, boy. And, Nigger, when are you going to school? Black and Brown men are not all in prison. Some Black and Brown men are free in some Black churches to worship and praise God. The Black churches need more ministry in jails and prisons as well. Some Black and Brown men serve God for two and half hours on Sunday, and some will not even go to visit other Black and Brown men on regular bases. Some institutions have so much red tape that many Black and Brown men get discourage to even try to visit those in prison. The Black church needs to stand up for civil rights, no matter what denomination you are with. The Black church needs to stand as one to be a pillar of the community. Slavery in Black and Brown men had church and gospel songs brought them through tough times.

The mind is a terrible thing to waste, and most of our people are wasting away. When people come into knowledge of things and their surroundings, they become powerful and able to withstand the onslaughts of society. *From the Womb to the Plantation to the Penitentiary* will capture the real deal in America and its real radical approach on racism. I hope and pray that whoever reads this book will understand the reality of some White Americans and the schemes that are used against our minority men. Lord, Lord, I need you to help me. This book is dedicated to the young men in my family and my church family as well. Keep the faith, and keep moving forward.

CHAPTER 1

THE BIRTH OF THE BLACK AND BROWN MAN IN SOCIETY

In the womb, you are created by the Almighty God, and your parents are the vessels to get you here. Freedom inside your mother's womb, you are covered from all outside influences of this unpredictable society. Patiently, you wait until that wonderful time when all hell breaks loose. Mother has broken her water, and the term has come for you to be delivered to this world. It does not matter whether you are full-term or premature; you still are a creation of God and all His glory. Also, coming through the birth canal can be a tug of war, or, if by chance there is a C-section, it can be very ugly as well. The delivery of birth is what God Himself has created, and no one—not even the doctor—can deny the process of this great thing to become a human being.

I personally have not given birth, but I have witnessed my two children, who are now grown-ups. The process of giving birth for a woman is a very serious matter. The process of young Black and Brown men living in their mother's womb is the learning of what is to come when the child is released from the womb. The mother and the father should feed the fetus and speak and talk to the fetus about the world before the child comes forth. The language they engage in with one another is personal between mother and father. Then when the time comes forth, the child can identify the parents. Just as Jesus states in

John 10:4 NKJV, "And, when he brings out his own sheep, he goes before them; and the sheep follow him, for they know his voice."

Training starts in the womb, and the preparation starts for life inside the womb of the mother, so the child or children have a sense of awareness in their birth pattern of life. As a parent of the modern world today, I am grateful for the chance to have spoken into my children's lives. I am still working on my relationship with my children and my relationship with God. I still believe that it takes a community to raise a child because all lives matter.

And when he brings out his own sheep, he goes before them; and the sheep follow him, for they know his voice. (John 10:4 NKJV)

The language of the Black and Brown men is something to deal with because it still portrays that they are, in some ways, still in their mother's womb. They can engage with one another such as a boy, and this means that some of them have not grown to manhood. Then some of them call their girlfriends "mama," and some call their place of dwelling their crib. These type of street language or Black English created in the environment of still being in the womb. The scene of baby mama drama and the scene of not getting a job or providing for their offspring makes it hard for them to be responsible in society. Then there is the environment that can cause ghetto fabulous drama as well, such as poverty and health issues and lack of motivation. Instead of working or going to school, some of these men would rather hustle on the streets. In this environment, some of these men would rather listen to negative degrading rap music that is putting all kinds of thoughts in some of their heads. Everyone wants to be a gangsta rap artist. Some of these men do not want to leave the womb.

A mother eagle has given birth to the nest, and as soon as they are chirping, they are getting their food and getting ready to fly. Now, when they begin to struggle as they fly, the mother swoops down under them and guides them a little until they don't have any problem flying. Animal behaviors have a fascinating way to help their offspring leave the nest faster than most human beings are capable of.

I would like to speak about the nucleus of the family of the Black and Brown men in America. Since the introduction of welfare, the government agency helped in some cases separate the nucleus of the Black and Brown family. Some Black and Brown men have been kicked to the curb. Now it is not always the agency's fault or the system's fault. Sometimes, it is the men themselves that create their own separation as well.

Some Black and Brown men fail to realize that selling drugs and committing crime are not the way to support and maintain a family lifestyle. There are some who are scared and have no real guidance on how to become a man and how to seek help with their wilderness experiences in life. I believe each man does have a wilderness experience in life, myself included. Some men will not reach out in times of trouble or tough times to other men. There are some reasons for that—some men do not trust other men to share their troubles with. Then there is the pride issue that some men carry that "I can do this by myself" not so.

Times out of the womb can leave some men hurting and angry in the world they live in. Then some of these men come back to the womb. "Mama, I need to come back home," or "Mama, can I come home?" Once you leave the womb, some men are able to maintain a decent lifestyle. But some men are labeled as "mama's boy," and some are always close to their mother because of that bond. Now on the other hand, the father means well, but some fathers still want to show the young man how to become a man.

"Get tough, and show what you are made of. No son of mine is going to be weak." Here is the conflict between mother and father in the home, the womb. Some of these Black and Brown men need to know that Mama and Daddy will not be here forever. Take what the womb or the home instructs you to do, and live a decent life. Just like the mother eagle, the parents are there to guide you when you fall or fail. For some men, this is a hard lesson to learn, no matter how many times some men continue to fail. In the book of Proverbs 22:6 NKJV, it states, "Train up a child in the way he should go. And when he is old he will not depart from it." In the womb or the home, the Black and Brown man should receive some good instruction on how to maintain a decent lifestyle.

Sometimes, some Black and Brown men can receive some good advice and some sound wisdom, but it is also good to carry it out to work out things with God in their wilderness. Life is not always nice and pleasing, and some people are not as positive as they claim to be. Sometimes, Black and Brown men may try too hard and fail and don't have a strong support base to help them out. There is no father figure in their life or uncle, big brother, and church deacon to help them with their struggles.

In my own struggles, I have learned how to ask for help, and I have learned how to accept it as well. In the process of the womb separation to the wilderness, we as Black and Brown men need to trust God and believe. Not many of us Black and Brown men trust God at all simply because of our heritage and experiences. As we come from the womb, we as Black and Brown men sometimes become slaves to the environment we have to live in. Some men may feel "This is all I am cable of" and "This is all I will ever be." Some Black and Brown men can lose sight of their potentials. They must know and believe that they can be all they can be.

Once out of the womb, some of us Black and Brown men need to realize that society has given you a strike for your identity. You are young, gifted, and Black and Brown men. The same Creator created society, so why do some White Americans see otherwise? This label of some Black and Brown men has been said that we are lazy and unwilling to learn or to do better. Black and Brown men have a disadvantage before they can even walk. The development of some Black and Brown men has a radical effect on society in the way some of us are still holding on to the womb. Society will not hold you down; it will only give you the playing surface you need to maintain your lifestyle. People judge most of the time about our race and our accomplishments. No matter the neighborhood, you still are an American citizen.

As I grew up in the intercity projects (because that was what they were— projects), the population in the city had grown during the sixties. People of color had to be placed in the projects. The high-rise places were not always the greatest places to live in. The government had a plan by design to keep certain people of color in certain locations throughout certain areas in the city. Once again, if you were in this type of communities, you were labeled as working-class people. My family used this community as a stepping stone to do better and move on to a better community. This took place because of the murders of Malcom X and Dr. Martin Luther King Jr. Certain people in high places in the United States of America felt that these men were causing trouble in America when these men of color were only expressing their civil rights to speech and their civil right to protest the unjust in American society.

The government of America was very concerned about the uprising of the Black and Brown men in America. They were beginning to see the true colors of America for what it was at that time in history. The Black and Brown men had a driven purpose to seek the knowledge and the education of what was going on in America. These men were killed for what they believed and tried to show—that the Black and Brown men were still being used as slaves in the society of America. These men wanted to wake up the Black and Brown men to their own identity and culture as a race of people. I know God is a God of variety because he made all humanity. He is the creator of life. Man can and will soon cause destruction on this planet because of his hidden motives and bias of people of color. Black and Brown men of this country were not immigrants; they were captured by greedy White men, who had unjust reasons to enslave these men of color.

In this situation, the road is tough, and no doubt the going gets rough and the hills are hard to climb. But we, as Black and Brown men, were given tough and rough treatment throughout our heritage, and we as a people still continue to survive. Some Black and Brown men don't even remember why they are free today. There are some of them who are lost and have no driven purpose in their lives. Some of them live with their women who act like their mamma and cannot function without her at all. They are less encouraged to get a job and live off her and her social services money—still living in a crib and still not living in a house or an apartment of their own.

The Black English that is spoken is so broken in our society that White America plays on their intellect and the way they speak to one another. Then there is the dress code and hairstyle, and the language again is very rough indeed. Where do we go from here? Lord, Lord, I need you to help me. The Black and Brown men need to help the younger ones to grow up better and keep their minds focused on their driven purpose in life. Now don't get me wrong. There are Black and Brown men doing this in their community, and they are doing very well. But those men who use other men as parasites, those are the ones I am speaking to. Help our condition, and help our cause as a people of society because we are almost an endangered species.

Today, there are some Black and Brown men who still in the womb—not literally speaking, but they will not move out, and mama will not encourage them sometimes to move out. They become mama's boys, and they struggle to move out. Once the pattern is set in the upbringing in the home for some Black and Brown men, they seem not to even want to move out. Now, most of the time, the father is not there, and Mama really has no support to motivate the young man out of the house. The fathers of some of these men don't really know about encouraging their own sons because no one really helped them in their own lives as they were growing up. So we have the domino effect that is carried over to the next generation, and when that happens, some of these young men don't really grow up. I believe a change of environment will help some of these young men to strive and get a better outlook on life.

The mind and the biological makeup of the Black and Brown man is strong and vibrant. That's why in slavery, the Black and Brown men worked in the fields. The White men and the native American could not work in the plantation fields. We need to always be reminded in sports and in the political world how we are developed as free men in society. Let us remember that, yes, we are born of the womb, but we are never to stay in the womb. Yes, society and all the cultural racism that we face as men will probably never change, but we as men must strive to continue our quest as free men on this Earth to overcome our stigma—the stigma of being not equal to the White counterpart in this American society.

The level of institutional slavery or racism is an educated game or process to undermine some of the Black and Brown men in America. Some of us have fallen to this game and not even really realizing it. Once we as men of color leave the womb, we are to be inspired to learn more about the schemes and new revolutionary schemes that will come. Will racism and the process ever leave America? Or will there just be better ways to cover up the systemic process of racism? Leaving the womb can be scary for some of us, but it is a challenge that is needed to be met. With all the negative activities that's been done to us, we must keep marching on. I need to ask the question, "How do you value your freedom?" Freedom to the Black and Brown men should inspire us to live on for our very survival.

As I continue to get deeper into the study of this book, I want to inspire all men who are struggling with the "womb concept" to break loose from the stigma that enslaves you. Young men need to open up their minds and realize this is a true fact about some Black and Brown men who need Mama right there and right now. The womb concept is a stigma to our young men and our seasonal older men as well. The older men must teach the younger men about the struggles and tribulations that we as a people went through.

I had the chance to visit the Black Wax Museum located in Baltimore Maryland. There was exhibits of all African Americans of all complexions. They have done great works for this American society. They have Black and Brown inventors that have creatively helped with the medical and judicial fields of America. Still today, some of these men of color have not been given the recognition that they should receive as creative thinkers in America. The womb does have a process of creating thinkers and doers of society, which is good. However, the womb can create a curse for such Black and Brown men of color in our society.

Back in the Garden of Eden, God created man and woman, but once this couple disobeyed God, the struggles began. Man must work by the sweat of his brow of the land. The woman will have pain and tribulations giving birth. Genesis 3:9–19 explains the whole concept of the womb. The absolute disobedience of God caused a generational curse to the womb.

Now in the twenty-first century, we have a similar curse of the womb of these Black and Brown men. The father, once again, is not always around for whatever reason, and the child or children have some mentally or distributing illness from birth. Some of these Black and Brown men have been diagnosed with autism, mental-learning disorders, and other traumatic issues that are coming out at birth. Can the parents be partially to blame, or can this be hereditary? Whatever the case, these Black and Brown men have been labeled already and have been put into special agencies that are claiming to help with their social disabilities.

There are agencies and drug treatment centers for youth with crack baby births and alcoholic births. There may be some help with this epidemic. But by large, not enough is being done for this population in American society. They collect the moneys from various agencies such as DHS, SSI, and SSD. They will let the young Black and Brown men stay as long as they can to collect the money from the agency, and there is no follow-up once the individual is released. In my experience, I have worked in such an agency, which I dare not tell the name. There are certain polices they have in place that only help these individuals to fail simply because they have to go back to the same environment that have helped them get there in the first place. The therapist is usually White, and he or she probably have never experienced the traumatic issues of the womb. They have only studied it or read about it in a book or case study, but not in real life.

Now as a parent of two adults, children's behavioral patterns start as soon as they can walk—about ten months to eleven months old. This stage of change has to be watched and observed by both parents because it is both the genes of the parents that produced the child or children. The young mind is busy exploring everything they can in the home environment. Even in church, some of these young people are not easy to handle. Now while they are growing up in their environment, they take on the struggles, problems, and concerns of the household. Remember, Daddy's not always there, or if he is there, in some cases, there is no influence or help. The son starts to try to provide for the family, and he really doesn't want to work or go to school, so he picks up the street life. The hustle for drugs and other criminal activities come along in such an environment.

The womb creates an environment that is safe and protective for the young that is about to be born of the flesh. But once the child is born to the environment outside the womb, the child takes on a totally whole new character. The child needs to adapt to the surroundings of all that is near for survival. Now the child can be born with birth and learning defects that can make this child's environment hard to adapt to. However, once this offspring finds ways and means to adjust, the child begins to learn how to survive in their environment. The tools that these young Black and Brown men learn are not always tools that are accredited to learning in such an environment. When they grow up and there is no father figure, some of these men take on the responsibility to bring home money to help out their mother. The mother may be struggling, and the young male wants so badly to help his mother by any means necessary. So some of these young men of color take to streets. They think it is better to do these things that can earn fast money as the way to go, hustle, and build a security nest for the family.

We know in America, everything is not secure. The computer age is so modernized with new software that there is room for more and more corruption through the internet. You cannot always believe some of the stuff that happens, but you need to be mindful of the evil that lurks inside these computers in our society. These computers are made for good, but in the wrong hands, they are deadly as a smoking gun, which brings me to another question, "How do these guns and drugs get into the Black and Brown communities, and who is suppling these items?" The question is still and quiet, but the answer my friends is blowing in the wind. This involves the Black and Brown men and some communities in this country to get into street gangs. Some of these Black and Brown men look for comfort and want to be a part of something for protection in these mean streets. They believe some of them cannot stand alone or really be on their own from the corruption of these mean streets. There are some false beliefs that they may take on to only survive in the intercity streets and maintain a family. They are soldiers of misfortune in the environment that they live, and they carry out their handiwork in the community. Then most of them are caught by the police—only when there is an election year. The crime rate has skyrocketed, and then the police wants to get tough on the war of drugs. Only when a political figure is trying to clean up the streets and wants votes from the community and church leaders to better the community do we as people hear from them. Lord, Lord, I need you to help me.

The womb in the nucleus of the Black and Brown man should have the support of both parents in the picture. But sometimes, that is not always the case. I believe that the nucleus of the family in the community of the Black and Brown men has to be built on spiritual and historical foundations. Every Black and Brown family does not have the same foundation when it comes to the nucleus of the family. The systemic racism in this country has put their make to break some of these families in the communities of Black and Brown men. The struggle goes on in America for better education, jobs, voting, and housing. Civil rights and all that is part of this stigma in America has to stop. When will it stop, no one knows, but we can cry out and spare not about the injustice of this country called America. People of the world, we are living in a ball of confusion, and the only thing that can come of this is when Jesus Christ is to come because He is to come. We know that all lives matter, and so do Black and Brown men's lives. The unity has to come for all Americans now. The pandemic is here. Lord, Lord, I need you to help me. The struggle for the Black and Brown men is still paramount in the United States. The present time that we are in is a greater struggle because we are in a pandemic, social injustice, systemic racism, and economic trouble. These are tough situations and hard times for some of the Black and Brown men to grapple with.

THE LEVEL OF EDUCATION

What is Education? The American Heritage Dictionary describes education as the knowledge or skill obtained or developed by a learning process. The process of learning for the Black and Brown men comes from the environment and the home. Once again, whether or not both parents are there, the beginning of education starts at home. There are two levels of education in the minority race. There is the classroom and the streets. The classroom is where Black and Brown men must adapt in learning the bylaws of our society. The streets are where Black and Brown men learn to adapt in the society.

The classroom of learning is set up to benefit those who can complete and are willing to learn in such a setting of education. This teaches discipline, academic awareness, social behavior and how to behave in a social setting. The classroom is also where some Black and Brown men learn character, but some may even find out that the classroom setting is not always helpful to them. Some Black and Brown men can complain that they cannot learn in such a setting. They feel confined, and some do not want to listen or sit still in the classroom. I believe the classroom to be inspiring and a rewarding place for educational achievement. However, there is the streets that give an easy way out of the classroom. The self-taught and the self- made person does not always need the classroom at times. That's when the struggles begin in their lives because some may refuse to go to school and choose the hustle of the streets to make their living.

Most of us know that in America, there is no real equal education for the Black and Brown youth. Some live in poverty and discomfort and have no backbone at home because some of them have no father and don't agree with the social system of education and work ethic for survival and well- being. The level of education in those neighborhoods does struggle even to just get to graduation of middle school. They just don't want to sit in a structural setting. They sometimes become uneasy, and they don't respect the environment of learning and discipline for their self-worth in society.

There seems to be a curse of generational behavior. They kill, many of themselves crime against one another. The truth of the matter is that Black and Brown women have strived to make life better for themselves with their level of education. They may have children or not, however, they manage, with the help of social programs that are willing to work with them. However, there are still some that don't get out of the rut and don't try at all to achieve the level of education. In the streets, there is no snitching and no ratting on anyone in the hood. This is also incorporated with the gangs in the streets, and there is no such thing as a good gang. The streets are a trouble, and no person can learn anything positive from the streets. The Black and Brown men of society cannot even build a future of economic standards from the streets of the hood. The standards are not legal, and they are corrupted and totally not honorable for our men. They can only make life worst for our young men, who come out of jail or prison. They claim that some of these men have no real ambition of learning or trying to learn. The street-gang life is dangerous for our young Black and Brown men.

Believe that as the weather climate changes, some of these young men's mental minds change as well. There are some of them that act as if they were in hibernation for the winter and break out in the spring and summer as gangsters on a killing spree. There is some mental illness that is encamped in their genetic makeup that causes violent and irrational behavior. I believe this is true. As an experienced retired case manager for the parole and probation population of young Black and Brown men, some of them are on heavy medications. The type of medication keeps them from their violent and irrational behaviors. They may function normally and have the skills to do what is right, but if you forget to give them their medication, there will be hell to pay. The mental illness in some of these Black and Brown men I believe is triggered by the climate in certain cities or by the atmosphere.

The term "turnup" is the reason to break wild and cause havoc in the community. Now, there are agencies and places for some of these men that claim they are helping them, but all they do is give them medication and keep their emotions and their thinking under control. These agencies in our society try to help, but most of these young Black and Brown men have no family support or no support at all. They suffer because they are victims of the streets. The power is in the hands of the community, families, the educational leaders, and our local churches. The power lies in the hands of the community leaders and the voters who are registered and who care about these Black and Brown men in our society.

The people have the power to vote. Most Black and Brown men really don't care to vote. They feel that the elections are fixed and that money talks and bullcrap walks. Then there are these secondhand citizens. Those who are on parole cannot vote. This has changed in some states. Now, people who are on parole can vote if they choose to do so. Still, they believe that they cannot get decent housing and a decent job. The chances for them will end up on welfare, SSD, or SSI. Society really does not give ex-offenders much of a choice. They mostly pay for child support and payments back to the state where they have committed a crime. This is so hard for some of these men because they suffer not to go back inside if they fail not to pay for their debt to society. Freedom certainly comes with a price. Society will allow them to maintain their freedom as long as they stay in their boundaries and curfew limitations. Once these men are released from prison, the caseworker and the parole department work together to release these men to halfway housing or shelters in certain communities. However, depending on the crime these men of color have committed, they are placed right back where they have committed their offense. From sex-offenders to murders on parole, they have certain communities they are allowed to live in.

Everyone in life has made mistakes, and some continue to make mistakes, and they have issues in their life. How do we as people wake up to a system that is set up in some cases for them to fail? Black and Brown men are almost 90% of the prison population in some states of America. But the scope of the matter is that the development of these young men comes from the nucleus of the family—their family. Some families are built on tradition, and some families are built on the modern ways of life. Some families are spiritual, and others are not. However, the nucleus of the family should be the basis for the moral fabric of society where they live in. Nevertheless, certain Black and Brown men who lived on the wild side and do not have any regard for morals of a decent nucleus family in the society where they live are doomed to suffering in the worst way. I believe, with the help of the community and all the powers that are mentioned earlier, these men can get the help they need.

There are three rows for the Black and Brown men to maintain. The courtroom, after the conviction of a crime, the defendant is seated in the front row. He will always remember his crime and will face whatever sentencing in front of a judge and jury. The time in his mind that he must serve to get it right is at the front row of his life now. Time waits for no one, and time is moving right after the verdict. Then there is the front row in the funeral gathering. The front row in the church or the pallor itself is the front row. The Black or Brown man is laid out in the coffin and is confronted with death. The body is stiff and cold. The family is suffering because of the lifestyle this young man has been living, good or bad. The preacher tries to do a good job of the eulogy. The preacher tries to console the family as well. But the family seated at the front row knows the truth about the deceased. How could this have happened, you say? Well, look at the moral fabric of the nucleus of the family. No matter how this happened, look at the nucleus of the family.

Then there is the front row for the graduate. The Black or Brown man has completed the educational goals set by the nucleus family. The front row of graduation does not always protect the graduate from the other two rows;

they can pop up at any stage of growth in the young man's life, Black or Brown. Equally important is the moral and tight fabric of the family, which can also drive this graduate to the wild side of people, places, and things in life because of the pressures to do good. In certain families, this can happen. The parent means well, and they try their best, but the graduate wants to take a trip on the wild side to explore and see what it is like. Then once the young man has been hurt, how should society forgive him? Jesus states in Colossians 3:13 NIV, "Bearing with one another, forgiving one another, if anyone has a complaint against another: even as Christ forgave you, so you also must do." Let us truly remember that we as a society need to always have compassion and respect for those men who have fallen and are able to get back up again.

To continue on the scripture and the three rows of the Black and Brown man's life, my prayer is that all society can have true forbearance and transparency to the young and old men of color who have fallen to the wilds of society's evil. I believe that no one is exempt from sin. Some choose not to sin, and some make the choice to sin. The Bible here is the guide about sin, stated in Romans 3:23 NKJV: "For all have sinned and fall short of the glory of God." Once again, we all have fallen short and are sinners saved by the grace of God. I have sinned, and I know how to have compassion and respect for my fellow man. The transparency is in the scriptures and not always in what comes out of the mouths of certain believers, whether they are in church, work for the church, or are true worshippers of the church. Christ did it all for us on the cross, and we, as true people of God, should have true transparency for the Black and Brown person that has fallen and struggled to get back up to live.

The three rows in the Black and Brown man's life comes with a variety of life situations. I must go back to the three rows. The nucleus of the family is the front line or beginning of how the three rows comes about. Depending on the lifestyle of the Black and Brown man's family, upbringing should help with the makeup of the behaviors of the three row situations. I know that these three rows have a force that comes from developing the characteristics of the Black and Brown man in all seasons of his life. Row number one consists of criminal behavior and social disorder. The Black and Brown man has one strike against him in this society because of his makeup or DNA. Why does this stigma carry such a burden on the face of the Black and Brown man? Because some of the White counterparts have developed some type of racism in the nucleus of their own family upbringing.

The three rows of the Black and Brown men's life have helped to develop the pattern of some to these Black and Brown men as I demonstrate the stigma and racial culture of our American society. Number one, come on down. He is the next contestant on the front row. The charge is robbery in third degree. The Black or Brown man has been indicted of robbery in third degree. The court room is mostly White, and none of his peers is able to be there. The public defender is representing the defendant. The deck is already stacked against the one who is being sentenced. The defendant has maybe one or two family members, and that is about it. Cool and clammily, the defendant awaits his fate in the eyes of the judge. Then after the prosecution and the defense have words, the verdict comes down as guilty as charged. The Black or Brown man is handed his fate, and he is saddened for doing what he did. But what could make this person such a bad person at this time? Could it be the nucleus of the family, or could it be that he had a drug problem that led to this ugly crime? How could the mighty have fallen? Then the Black or Brown man is led away to serve three years in state penitentiary. Then there is the climate of the crime. Could this be a crime of the weather in the community? These are all possible causes of this crime for this individual. No matter what, nobody is greater than God.

Then there is the second row. The funeral of the Black or Brown man as he is laid to rest. The second row shows the life of this Black or Brown man and how he lived young and or old. The setting could be a church or a pallor. The person is laid out in his coffin, and the song "Amazing Grace" is playing. As people view the body of the individual, one would wonder what really happened to this person. Is this person a drug dealer? WIs this person shot by a police officer? WIs this person sick, mentally and physically? Whatever the case, the second row is where life is ended, and death has entered, and now, one must begone from this life. How do you begin to accept death in the second row? Is this a good person, or is this a bad person? The preacher has the task to do the preparation of the eulogy and the task to console the family at the same time. He must put all negativity about this person to rest. The preacher must capture true transparency and have a good conscience on what he will deliver in this homegoing of the Black or Brown man. You know, some are saying that Black and Brown men are becoming a lost species. Yet the second row, for whatever the loss of life Black and Brown men have to be considered not living very long. Remember the song "Amazing Grace."

Then there is the front row of graduation. This is about the achievements of the Black or Brown man and the goals he has set out to do by the nucleus of the family—the graduation from high school to college or from college to higher learning. Let us not forget it is the nucleus of the family and the moral goals that set the stage for the graduation of this Black or Brown man in America, motivating him to achieve these goals and stand tall in his achievements. In humble recognition, I know what it takes for some of these Black and Brown men to get to the level of graduation. It can be hard without support, and it can be easy if there is the right guidance in life. There are many Black and Brown men in American history that did not always have a silver spoon in their mouth. Some have gotten help from others, and some had to work hard and stay focus. So now, as we close out this chapter, I will always remember that much is given and much is required with total compassion and transparency. In this twenty-first century, I hope and pray that we as a people can live freely and will not have stigmas against one another. We need to live together.

CHAPTER 3

INSIDE A JAIL CELL UNIT

Inside a jail cell unit, I have the honor to interview an inmate by the name of G. He does not really want to use his real name. I told him that is okay with me. He tells me that Black and Brown men are trying to make the best of the situation that they are in right now, waiting on time to pass. These men and other men inside are struggling with everyday life to survive. By the way, G is Black. And my local church has a jail ministry that can allow for this interview to go on. G states that some men work out, some play card games, some play checker or chess, and some have Bible studies. The White inmates try to take control as trustees to set up a type of system on the inside so they can be protected by the correction officers.

However, G states that this is only a temporary thing because some go home and others may or may not replace the ones that left.

As I observe, the whole system has a structure for all races of people. Most of the inmates are respectful and kind. The bottom line is no one wants to be there. "The public defender is a joke," G states. "He tries to reduce your charge and works alongside the DA, who lies about the grand jury indictment when it takes a while before the grand jury can indict you. It takes about ninety days before they can, and you are put in jail until they do or they don't." The railroad starts to move. There are smart men with degrees in jail. They have made some bad choices, just like G has made. I had the chance to speak to some preachers and some church people who are on the inside. They have the "have" and the "have-nots" as well. There are favorites, just like anywhere else.

People are not perfect and don't always try to remember where they come from. The world is a ghetto, and it is terrible, and the "haves" are always on the "have-nots," even in jail as I observe. Guys hustle just like they are on the streets or in their own hood. You cannot trust anyone in jail or prison, so don't make any friends or relationships that will come to harm you. The atmosphere is calm, and the mixture of people seems to be cool. The gambling table is flowing.

I just observe G working out, and he is going to take shower before my visit. I wait patiently as I start the time with G. For this session, G wants to share that he is tired of coming in and out of jail. He believes that society has put secret police in place to stop Black and Brown men in their tracks. G has two young sons that he hopes to see soon, and he wants to be with them. He wants to be a better father and a better person to deal with their upbringing. Life can bring all sorts of trials and tribulations. It is how we deal with the trials inside a jail cell. I can understand that my nephew is going through the same problem. Black and Brown men living together must make the best of their situation, waiting on time to pass. They struggle with the everyday survival in jail. As for G, he can also identify with this same situation. Some work out, some play cards, some play checkers and chess, and some just play games. The White inmates try to take control as trustees to stand out and be different from the rest, but at the end of the day, they are inmates too.

The whole system has been structured, from what I am told by G, for all races of people. Most of the inmates are respectful and somewhat kind because of the crimes they have committed. The bottom line is that no one wants to be there. "The public defender is a joke. He tries to reduce your charge and works alongside the DA, who lies about the grand jury indictments when it takes a whole three months before anything gets done, and you just sit inside with no bail." The railroad is trying to start to move. There are smart men with degrees in jail. They all have made some bad choices, just like some preachers, some deacons, some lawyers, and some congressmen as well. The law has its favorites, just like anywhere else. People are not perfect and don't always try to remember where they come from. The world is terrible and the "haves" are always on the "have-nots," even in jail. Guys hustle just like if they are on the streets or in their own neighborhood. "You cannot trust anyone in jail or prison," G says. "So don't make any friends or relationships that will cause you harm." The nature of the jail is calm. The mixture of the people seems to be cool. The gambling table is flowing.

I just finished my interview with G. I prayed to God to start my Bible study with some of the inmates after lunch. Some men come down to the Bible study that is in place. We pray and we discuss the forgiveness that God has given each man in the circle of life. The men seem to encourage one another and give hope on the situation they are in. This is a very good study. There are factions in this fifty-three-man pod, and all are trying to outdo each other in competition for space.

There is a young man in a wheelchair. They call him "hot wheels." He is a thief. He will steal your food before you know it. He is twenty-five years old, with cerebral palsy. He is a sneak, and he watches your food tray for any deals he can make. People go for medical treatment and bring back messages from other inmates. They are called "mules" or "carriers." There are gang-related issues as well in this pod of fifty-three men. All I can do is observe and be calm. Respectful attitudes always help in this situation and can carry you throughout the day. God has protected this pod that seems to be in the lion's den. I am reminded that all people of all color are not perfect. We struggle in our flesh, and we struggle with life issues. We try as a people to be patient with one another for things we need to survive with one another. In this pod is a little city. Life is tough, and there is diversity in every cell. People need people to survive even in jail. It does not matter what you have done or how old you are. Some people in jail only seek instant satisfaction for their situation.

Society has a great impact on inmates when they get out. Depending if you are on parole or probation, life can be tough. Some of these guys have been repeaters of their crimes and have more than two felonies. In the mix of things, I have heard stories about child molestation, rape, assaults, robbery, murder, grand larceny, as well as mismeaners and other petty crimes. However, most of them claim they are innocent. No one is guilty right now, and no one will admit to it in the court of law. People in jail learn much of the legal system. If you did not know the law, you will know the law when you have committed a crime. Doing something out of character in life circumstances causes people to act up and turnup. I believe it is the weather climate that allows men of all races to cause mayhem and social unrest in some of their lives. When it is cold, things seem calm and not much crime is committed. On the other hand, when it gets warm, things happen and things changes.

Some Black and Brown men are not happy with their lives and act out what they don't want to do. The mental and moral things become a struggle, and some turn to drugs and alcohol to try to solve their problems. In jail or prison, people don't judge you for what you have done. God is the final judge and jury. Our society condemns, vanishes, puts out, and determines who stays in and who stays out of our jails and prison system. Some of the local churches will try these tactics to dishonor the person. They all are praying for you, and at the same time, they are condemning you. Romans 3:23 states that there is no distinction "since all have sinned and fall short of the glory of God." This includes bishops, pastors, elders, ministers, missionaries, deacons, trustees, lay people, and even those who are not in the church—those in high places, like the president, the pope, and all other governments of the world. So in jail or prison, we don't judge anyone. I know I am a sinner saved by grace, and I know that God is not finished with me yet. He loves us all and those who believe in Jesus Christ.

I want to go back to this special scripture in 2 Timothy 4:16–18, which says:

> At first my defense no one took my part: all deserted me. May it not be charged against them.

But the Lord stood by me and gave me strength to proclaim the word fully that all the Gentiles might hear it. So I was rescued from the lion's mouth. The Lord will rescue me from every evil and save me for his heavenly kingdom. To Him be the glory for ever and ever. Amen.

This scripture touches the heart of all men who have been put in jail or prison. When you don't have money, real love, and anyone, not even a wife to support you, and you do something out of character, nobody wants to bother with you. The only thing a man can do when he is down is to look up to God. In his cell, with his thoughts and with God, man can feel His spirit. The spirit of God can activate the mind and glide him to move on. God will protect and provide for you when you are in the lion's mouth. I know I have committed a crime out of character, and my addiction is part of it as well. God is my help, and He has helped me in my present depressed state.

Some of the people of God, as I have stated earlier, will always be quick to say, "I will pray for you." But some of them will never come to visit you, and some will not even call you. They say, "Tell him to call." The leaders will not even call you. Some of the people of God do not really even care. Some of them don't care if you are poor and broke. The leaders of the church will try to help you, but they, too, will talk to you like you are worth nothing.

No one knows how a man feels until you have walked in his shoes. I am sorry for the lies and things that I have done. I have been restored to God, and I am grateful every day of my life.

Nobody is greater than God. In my experience, God has kept me humble and has given me compassion for people who have gone through some tough things and has shared them with me. I will always keep, in true confidence, their stories of God. The lion's den can also be equal to the character of Job. Job was an upright man of God. God allowed Satan to take his family and all that he had. The devil wanted to see if Job would curse God. Job stated in Job 1:21, "Naked I came from my mother's womb, and naked shall I return: The good Lord gave, and the Lord has taken away: blessed the name of the Lord."

And now, I can feel like that of brother Job's at times. However, the bright side is that after he suffered for a while, God blessed him one hundred fold. I know that this journey wasn't going to be easy and hard times come, but you must trust, believe, and have faith in the Lord. God will deliver His promises. Life can give you some ups and downs. You may even feel you want to end it all, but don't lose faith in God because without faith, it is impossible to please Him.

In the jail ministry, there are ministers that can be a good messenger, and then there are some who are in wolf's clothing. We as believers must be aware of our spirit and have discernment. Every man on this fifty-three-man pod has been in the lion's den, one way or another. The thing is not to fall into the trap of wickedness. Holiness is right, and all have to strive to maintain the lifestyle of holiness. From the womb to the plantation to the penitentiary, men of all colors have to learn the way of God. The front row in some of their lives are only court rooms. Some of these men have not really grown up to manhood. They have lived off a woman or called themselves pimping off a woman, and then they are stuck in the plantation simply because some of them cannot find any other way than selling drugs or prostitution.

Then there is the level of education. Most of these men don't really want to go to school because they will rather make money on the streets. Then they are stuck in the planation once again. Some of these men live off stories and struggles that they only know. Some of these men don't get to see what is really out there in the world beyond Joseph and Clinton Avenues. Still stuck in the plantation are the living quarters of some of these men—the jails and institutions of the city that they live in. The neighborhoods are rundown, and the care of housing is poor as well as education and job opportunities. People have the right to decent education and decent housing. Also, equally important is the chance for a good job with good wages. The tough part is that crime rates become high because they become predators in the neighborhood. The "have" and the "have- nots" are people basically trying to live in peace with each other. But the systemic government have them at each other for the right to survive. The poor has a hard time getting off the plantation.

I was in this type of drug plantation, and I was addicted to crack cocaine. I fell into a sea of darkness—no job and no money, with a habit. I would not even help out in the household. My companion seemed like she did not want me around. She did not want me to have anything at all. So I robbed a bank to support my habit. I almost got away with it, but the clothes I had on was my giveaway. So I was in jail, with a charge of robbery in third degree. The lawyer stated that I had a mental breakdown due to my drug use. My esteem was at an all-time low, and I was not myself at all. My record was good. I just was desperate, full of hurt, and acted out of character. I have learned a lot from this situation, and I will build on it and never will I get caught up again.

Everyone has some issues, and everyone has their day of Job in the lion's den. Job was special because he did nothing, and God allowed him to go through the tough and hard road. But for me, I caused my own issues when I became addicted to drugs. I can say that and I will always remember the process of healing as I do today. God has forgiven me, but some people of the local church have a hard time forgiving me. The Holy Spirit has given me insight not to worry about what was done. He has given me the strength to go on. I was fractured, and God fixed me. I will be at peace with my crime, and in a year's time, I will move on.

The Holy Land Jerusalem sounds like a nice visit. I would love to experience the place Jesus Christ travelled and study the landmarks where He ventured. I am always thankful for the angel God has given me. This angel is special and always gives me strength through prayer. Sometimes, I don't always listen or follow, but when needed, God provides a ram in the bush. This angel is special, and God has used the angel to cover and comfort me in tough times. I am grateful for this special angel in my spiritual life. I believe everyone has an angel that watches over them in hard and good times. In this spiritual life, the enemy is powerful and strong. The enemy is capable of changing at any minute the cares of life. How we handle our mistakes and problems will determine the growth of our spiritual life.

Some people think money will solve all our problems. But money will not solve all our problems, but it will help to have some. Desperation and anxiety can play mind games on the individual's mind. Mental anguish and low esteem can cause defeat in one's life. But God, who can cover you with angels of mercies, is a great God. Nobody is better than Him. Black and Brown men in this situation really struggles in this life. Incarceration is really hard for some Black and Brown men. While some can adapt in the environment of jail, others cannot. For whatever reason, some Black and Brown men choose to stay on the plantation, and it is not too good. Maybe they have become institutional as slaves to their own crimes and addictions and cannot stop using. Or maybe this what some of them settle for as men of color. I do not agree. I believe that life can be better for Black and Brown men if they choose to do so. The healing of the fractured man can get—and will be—better if only he trusts and believes that God can fix him. In Jesus's name. Amen.

Gene pigments occurring in the skin, hair, or retina of human beings and many animals (melanos creek black).

Melanism is the darkness color resulting from an abnormal development of melanin in the skin, hair, and eyes of a human being, or in the skin, coat, plumage of an animal.

THE BLACK CHURCH

The Black church in certain areas of our society has shown some contradictory methods when it comes to Black and Brown men and White men of our society. The younger men stated that they have a problem with some preachers. They say some of them not all believe that preachers are organized pimps, and they are pimping off the people of God. These young men are looking at the material things instead of the need of the preacher. Some of these Black and Brown men I have talked to don't quite get the spiritual aspect of the livelihood of the preacher of the gospel.

In this modern society, people of all races know that it does take money to run the ministry of God. The people know this, and the preacher knows this, but some people still don't get it. "The modern-day Black church is different from the church that brought our ancestors through slavery." The gospel helped a lot of Black and Brown men survive many lynching and killings in the old days. However, today, some churches have what is called "performances." They put on a show for the people of God, get them happy and in the spirit, and before you know it, you have given all your money away. Some of the Black churches have a zeal for souls, and the Black church has biblical testimonies that God can bring you through any situation possible. There is nothing too hard for God.

The Black church is the pillar of the community. When some Black and Brown men get in trouble, it should be the church of that community that would help them. However, this is not always true. Certain churches will turn their backs, or certain churches will forget about those who are in jail or in prison. Jesus states in Matthew 25:36, "I was naked and you clothed me; I was sick and you visited me; I was in prison and you came to me." How many Black churches have ministries as such? How many Black churches care enough to carry out this gospel? Some people in some of these churches are not all there in the spirit of God. People use preachers, and preachers use people. Some churches try to work the preacher to death and don't mind doing it. In the same manner, the preacher will do it to the people.

The preacher has the church building, and it is need of repairs, and he will come to the people. In fact, every time there is a fund raising for the church, the people are the first to be asked. Instead of asking the people of the church, the church should have other solutions to help with maintaining and repairing the church. Equally important is that some Black churches are standing still. There is no growth in ministry and no growth in the church. The young graduate moves on, the old gets old and die off. In certain churches, no one is trained or motivated to carry on the ministry in some of these Black churches. A change needs to come. As to when, I don't know, but certain churches can burn you out, dry you up, and kick you to the curb. The culture of Black and Brown men are also intertwined with the music of gangsta rap music. Some of these men have not finished school, and some don't even want to try. They are talented, and they are smart—but only street-smart. The Black churches are not always ready to receive them and their lyrics or messages. The language may be hard and tough, but the message is real. The society that we live in is racist and maybe cruel in the eyes of many Americans. The music in the churches and in the streets have a similar flavor and may have the same message, but they have a different audience to sing to.

I had a conversation with a gentleman about the church. He asked me if I was saved. I asked him, "Saved by grace or saved by the power of

God?" Then he mentioned that he was of apostolic faith. He mentioned one God, one faith, and one baptism. I knew right away that he was quite sure of the trinity: God the Father, God the Son, and God the Holy Spirit. When I mentioned the trinity, he looked somewhat puzzled. He stated the Jesus is God and they are one, but he did not mention the Holy Spirit. He stated that one God, one faith, and baptism is his doctrine (apostolic creed). Now in Pentecostal denomination, they state that we believe the Bible to be the only and infallible written word of God. And in that statement of faith, they do mention God the Father, and God the son, and God the Holy Spirit to give an account of the trinity and cover all the personalities of the trinity as well. Now in some Black churches, it can be confusing to the Black and Brown men if they are not educated in the Holy Bible and their churches' creed or statement of faith.

Back to the younger generation's hip-hop and the gangsta rap culture, the only thing they believe in is music and making money. Some of these black churches cannot say that. They are saying that the streets and the hood are where things are at. The hustle and bustle of the ghetto and crime life is what will bring record deals and a new way of life, not the "Bible." Where is God? How can one have faith when there is money to be made in the streets and in the clubs? Black and Brown men need money, and they are stepped on, and everyone is about their lifestyles and trusts in God. Trust is God. The dollar bill states, "In God we trust." However, do we really trust in God when we don't have any money or any food, or when we have been broken down to the lowest level in our lives? That's when the culture of hip- hop and gangsta rap comes into play, and the band plays on. It plays on to the troubled and hard times of some of these Black and Brown men. The lives of these men, whether they are in jail or whether they are in the church, are crushed by some churches.

God is love, and if we are supposed to love one another, then how can we not support the brother or the sister who is in trouble or is hurt? I understand that many will say, "We are praying for you," if they are really praying for you. Keep in mind that we as Black and Brown men are measured by our bank accounts and what property we own. There is also the trust factor of everyone else in the life of the Black and Brown men. Trust is measured again by the wisdom and belief of the Black and Brown men. Love for God is love. Some churches will keep their distance when a brother falls into trouble. Once again, money and power are the tools that keep some men and preachers above other men. "If you scratch my back, I'll scratch your back." Lord, Lord, I need you to help me. The poor soul that needs the help really doesn't get it.

Some Black and Brown men really don't always agree with the church's hierarchy. Some Black churches use family and close friends in the ministry instead of people outside—the so-called clicks. Some people in church create "clicks" when they don't even know they have created it just by having some common interest among them, such as playing golf or cooking or just have the same political party.

Black and Brown men are all around town. These men hustle and bustle to try to survive in a town called the "plantation of the north." Still, they have hope. They have a driven purpose to strive and survive the ways of life. The Black and Brown men in prison or in jail are trying to live in the same <u>mode of production</u> on the inside. Some of these men are trying to live a life of lies and schemes of getting over one another. Some of them will hustle food and commissary items to survive, and they will try everything to communicate to the outside community.

Just as important, the Black church has its service to that same community. The goal is to reach all souls at any cost, no matter how hard it gets. Jesus Christ has no problem, so why should the Black church in the community have this problem? Can we ask ourselves this question? Does the Black church know the community? What type of methodology does the Black church have in place to reach the community? Is it really driven to win souls for Christ, or is it just a scheme to boost up membership for the church? There are always possible reasons for the growth of the church, but it does matter how the leader and the people of the ministry carry out the task. There should be a group effort, and it should be done in love and unity, not just burning out the few people that do work while others give orders or instructions.

Some church folk can destroy the ministry with protocol and traditions, crushing the believer with this and that, about dress codes, and spiritual bondage. They think that just because they are in high places, they can instruct you on how the spiritual dance works. They think they are more spiritual than you are, and they think that they are better than you. Also, some may say that they are praying for you, but they are really praying against you. The only approval that is needed is approval from God. All of God's children should be pleasing God and not man. In 1 Thessalonians 2:4 NIV, it says, "We are not trying to please men but God."

Black and Brown men need to know there's a world of difference between performing for people's approval and being free to minister to their needs because you know you already have God's approval. Striving for approval is like any other drug; you can never get enough of it. And like all junkies, you go crazy when it's withheld. It places you at the mercy of other people's opinions. And as a result, you live in an emotional roller coaster. That's not how God wants you to live. The Apostle Paul was free to speak the truth in love: to confront people or to be gentle with them. When someone told Paul they did not like him, he did not lose sleep over it because his security and self-worth weren't built on their acceptance. It says in 1 Thessalonians 2:4, "We speak as men approved by God."

Black and Brown men need to protect and keep their neighborhoods safe from all harm and danger. It is equally important that we as men should not be enslaved in our minds of our limitations. Because when you are limited, people push you back and keep you down when you don't have anything to survive with. The people of this world are ugly, whether you are free or not. Most people claim to be honest and truthful, but most of all, the claim is some type of a scheme or disguise. As Black and Brown men, we have not always trusted the government and the slick ways of some politicians in our society. The declaration of independence states that all men are created equally. We know that this is not true. The Bible states that we all are God's children, and God is no respecter of person. Get the Scripture. Some of the Black churches don't really care for you unless you have money to give, and you can help change the church policy as well with money. Where are the some of the Black churches today? When a person falls, and no one really is brave enough to call and help lift that person up.

Paul didn't go around comparing himself with others, demonstrating his security and superiority by trying to be top dog or the one who's always in charge. Knowing he already had God's approval set him free from such anxiety, and it meant he could enjoy the life God called him to. When we're immature, we worry about what others think of us. But as we become more mature, we realize that most of the time, they aren't thinking about us at all. They're too busy thinking about themselves or worrying about what we think of them! Knowing you have God's approval gives you the strength to deal with criticism and conflict because you're secure in your identity. And your identity is this: You are redeemed, called, and approved by God.

Most Black and Brown men do not believe this because most of us are men of pleasures and we want to be accepted by men in power and men in authority, especially in the church. We need to stop showing off how much Holy Ghost we have, and instead, we need show how much love and compassion we have for our fellow man. The ministry for us people of color can make us traditionally tied down. There are things that go on in church that are not really Scripture-based. But people go on with it because they really think they are serving God and want to look good by doing it for the leader of the flock. The Black and Brown leaders of the church need to be sure that God has called them, and not man. The calling of the position of the church should be judged and called for by God. The statutes and the background of a leader do not always qualify men, Black and Brown or White, for God's ministry.

Jesse had several sons, and the youngest one was called to lead the children of Israel. King David was a shepherd over the sheep in the back hills of the land. So please remember, just because you are a servant under the bishop, this does not always mean you will always be a bishop. And just because the bishop gives you a church, this does not always mean you are indebted to him. You are always reminded to put God first and the ministry that God has equipped you to be in.

Some Black churches get caught up in so much honoring this and honoring that they sometimes forget to honor the Creator. There are churches in our society that really honor God, and they are nondenominational churches. Some denominational churches try to make you think they are about God's business and ministry, but they are really not. Now, I am not trying to discourage you about churches, especially Black churches. I'm just trying to let you know that there are good ones and ones that may lead some sheep astray. Remember this: you choose a church because of the spirit of God that dwells in that church—not for the choir, not for the preacher, nor the sound of the music. Keep in mind the ministry and the vision of the church and the Holy Spirit of God that dwells within the church.

Once again, some churches today do not share all the finances that go into maintaining a church or many churches. Money is the key in the modern- day church, and some people still believe that every penny is going into the church. There are people who read and search the Bible for answers for their own lives, but they never search and look for the truth in the modern church. Just because you are a pastor or just because you are a bishop, it does not mean you are above your flock. People are people when it comes to the power of men in high places that can change the focus of the people's perception of ministry. In the community of Black and Brown men, there are many viable options that come into play. There is a preacher on Sunday morning, who refers to the city as the "plantation of the north."

THE PLIGHT OF THE COMMUNITY

The plight of the community for some Black and Brown men is always in the mode of suffering to survive and to stay alive. Once again, the nucleus of the family plays an important part in most of these men's upbringing. The upbringing is so important because I believe that this can and will determine how most of these men will maintain a decent lifestyle. Mentally, these men must be able to go through the tough life living in a drug-infested neighborhoods. Most of them see the street's hustling and drugging as a lifestyle. Some of them even want to do just that. They are victimized by the games and hardships that play on in the street life. However, there are some who make it to the NBA or become preacher, a teacher, a banker, or even a civil rights activist. It is by design that they are placed in the social economic status of where they are, such as the low-income areas of our society.

There is also the "classes" in society that put the pressure on the Black and Brown men to survive. They have to be able to keep up with the pressures of succeeding when the deck is stacked against them. The blockbusting and the institutionalized racism goes along with the pressures of these men making it out of the ghetto. By design, in the early sixties, most of them and their families were placed in high-rise apartments and were sectioned off in the cities within USA. Racism can't be over. Some even when the different classes and the laws try to block these men of color. Yes, we shall overcome, but when? As we grow in population and technology, the changes and the worries of the world are pressured upon everyone. Some cannot really cope with the mental illness that has its hands on the mind of some of these men. The drug scene and all of its pleasures and deaths can cause—and will cause—some mental concerns among Black and Brown men. Not all these men are caught up in the web of this ugly situation. Some do make it, and others do come out of working class status. However, there are certain people in high places with rich hand, and they can influence our government to make laws to keep certain people in the poverty level.

There are other aspects of the plight of a community. The melting pot of different cultures that the Black and Brown men have to deal with to survive. There are the educational level and job level of the Black and Brown men. The Black and Brown men may not always have what it takes to get the right levels of education and the qualifications to get the jobs they want or need. The melting pot in the community is made up of many cultures and diverse atmosphere, and that change brings competition to the Black and Brown men. They must compete to make it or be discouraged in the community not to make it. The Black and Brown men must always work on their skills to better themselves and be able to advance in their mindset, not always settling for the bottom or not always being at the bottom of the totem pole. Then once again, there is the caste system that is setup in the culture of the Black and Brown men. This systematic class was created since slavery times by the White slave master and the special slave woman. Then the relationship created the mulatto or Creole. This was the moment of suffering in the Black race.

The darker you were, the farther you get the quality or equal way of living back in the sixties. This was a ruling stick of institutionalized slavery. People had to adjust to this lifestyle, especially if you had come from the south and did not adapt to the big city's community lifestyle, with all of its hang-ups and Jim Crow methods. The projects were a place that most of these Black and Brown men had to dwell in and live for some time. Once again, they were projects just to see how the Black community as a whole would live and survive. Also, there were other immigrants that lived in the hood. Some of them seemed to adapt quickly, and others seemed to go through the plight of the community.

People all over this country have been placed in certain areas by design, by political parties, and by certain ideologies. This is, by design, to keep confusion and racism continue in the United States of America. Most Black and Brown men do not live in the Midwest or in the central part of this country. Most of them live in the inner cities, and not many of these men are farmers as well. The plight of the community can bring about crime and destruction. The poverty level is low, and unemployment is high, and people cannot always get a job. Their education is low, and their self-esteem is low. I am talking about some Black and Brown men. These are the ones that have issues in the nucleus family. These are the ones who have issues with crime and drugs and also with economic survival. The streets add to the plight of the community. There is dope in almost every corner, and it's the very mindset of those who are hooked in drugs. They are not concerned about working. They are not eager to go to school. They are not looking for employment. Some of them (Black and Brown men) just wants the thrill of getting high. The systematic racism, drug trafficking, prostitution, and illegal gambling are crushing the community. The government may toss a lifeline but never a real cure for the sick Black and Brown men that are caught up in the job market and the education of life.

This vicious cycle of war on drugs or racism is controlling the minds of some of these Black and Brown men, who struggle with mental health and who sometimes cannot find their way out of a paper bag. There is a saying, "Stop blacks in their tracks," and there is also a saying, "Put it in a book, and they will never read it." This is simply because they won't read or pick up a book. Black and Brown men must become strong leaders in the community. They should become more politically involved. They need to get help from programs to help them. I know some are too proud or too macho to try new things. Life has many challenges for some of these Black and Brown men, and they really need help with the situation in the community they live in. Once again, the deck is stacked against them.

The plight of a community also involves the class system. There are upper middle class, middle class, lower middle class or the working class, and the lower working class, who needs to stay afloat. Each class has diversity within itself. These classes express the type of community level for the Black and Brown men who live in them. Out of the classes that were mentioned earlier, I would like to start with the lower class and work my way up to the upper middle class and the services that are provided in these communities. In the working class communities, I would like to focus on the type of services that are provided. In this class, the Black and Brown men's level of education, vocation, and living quarters are totally different from the upper middle class. For example, the type of education may be a high school or GED graduate level. The job may be a factory, automobile worker, postal worker, or a trade worker. The level of class is branded because of the level of housing and education. I live in the projects in Brooklyn, New York, and I am a Black man with a GED-equivalent education. I have no real level of seeking further education because this is who I am, and I live in the projects and have no potential to move up. I am then a stigma in my own community.

The level of services are low. The level of education is low. The housing is for low-income earners. The type of political representation is low. My self-esteem as a Black or Brown man is low. I am tired, and I hate my low- level job. The preacher at church tries to help, but my faith is low in God, and I cannot see my way out. I am stuck in a community that I hate. Lord, Lord, I need you to help me please! My mental health is low. I must drink to cope with my problems, and the more I drink, the deeper I become depressed. I really do believe in voting, and I don't really care. The plight is not in the community but in the Black and Brown men that make up the community. They need to pull together and become a unit that can become a power to work is the best interest of the community. The Black and Brown man needs to become politically connected, and the church needs to help and meet the needs of the poor, and those Black and Brown men must build up strong self-esteem and get the family involved. Then, with the help of social programs, they can get the community involved, one family at a time. The church should be the gathering place of the community, helping to keep the motivation and upward climb of many families in community. When God worked to settle the chosen Israelites, He established a community to survive in wilderness (look up Leviticus 19:9–37 in the Scripture). God provides for the widows and orphans. God's plan was to build a strong community for His people. So this community that the Black and Brown man lives in today is corrupted with violence, drugs, and prostitution, as well as with corrupt politicians, who only care about their reelection instead of the people who voted for them. This is the plight of the <u>lower working class </u>in the USA today, dealing with the pandemic or COVID-19. The classes above the lower working class really don't have as much problems—maybe not as much, but they do have some problems in their communities as well. The plight of the community is dangerous if the people does not stand to grow and survive. The upper middle class community does have the same problems as the lower working class. There is a song written by The Isley Brothers called "Fight the Power," and the lyrics say "you gotta fight the powers that be." These powers hold you down, have their foot on your neck, and will not allow you to motivate forward. You rise up out of poverty if you choose to, Black and Brown man. You can make a difference in your community! Get up and fight for the voting rights. Get up and fight the systematic racism in this community.

Black and Brown men, get up and stand tall amidst this COVID-19 pandemic and really care about our community.

SUMMATION

In summation, this book, *From the Womb to the Plantation to the Penitentiary* exhibits the trial and tribulations of the Black and Brown men from the local community up to the national levels of the civil rights movement. The Black lives matter, and all lives matter for cultural liberties in the nation. In the United States of America, Black and Brown men have to fight for all civil rights since 1954. I just want to name a few good men who have been on the battle field: Dr. MLK, Minister Malcolm X, John Robert Lewis, and President Barak Obama. These men have fought for civil liberties. Most Black and Brown men know that the Constitution, and the United States of America doesn't really stand for freedom for the Black and Brown men. Most Black and Brown men know that the declaration of independence really have no value because all men are not created equal. There is a stigma of social injustice and institutionalized racism in America for most of the people of color. Racism is like a cancer. It can become dormant, but then it can rise up when certain politicians get into office, they do things to set off social injustice. They stop the social programs and the economic climb of certain Black and Brown men. The education, the job market, the skills, and the knowledge of Black and Brown men become low. Some of them are blocked out of most social programs that can help them.

Now here's the part about the community at large for the Black and Brown men. Some of them chase the street life and get in the drug game and the hustle for fast money. They get caught up on using and selling. Some of them get caught up on gangsta rap music, which dictates their flair of music. This music also helps some Black and Brown men gain courage to face the everyday pressures in society or in their community. We as a people know who put the drugs in the community, and we know why—to keep Black and Brown men from fighting and killing each other off. This is a form of genocide.

We know whose children are going to Ivy League colleges and whose children are not. I am deeply saddened at the road that most Black and Brown men have to go through, myself included. I am not a racist. I was not brought up in a prejudice household. I learn about racism and social injustice when I went to school, and I was called a nigger in high school. People of all creation should know that God created all people for His purpose and glory. The journey is still not over, and the road is getting tougher. The hills are still hard to climb. I know, by the grace of God, we shall overcome this someday. This is continuously ringing in my ears. The Black and Brown men are not endangered species.

Then there is the border issues with people of color. They really have no clue on what to do with the border situation. We have a big crisis on our hands.

We came from one of the richest countries of the world—Africa. We came from where God created man. We came from royalty, and we're of strong people until slavery. So in this country, we remember the Holocaust. We should remember that Black and Brown men are not immigrants. Black and Brown women were also taken, with the help of some of the Africans. This was a plot designed to harvest and capture a culture of people to become slaves in America.

Black and Brown people are always strong and special. The melanin gene in our culture allowed us to work in the plantation fields back in the early stages of America—the economic climb. The Indian or Natural Americans could not do it. The White counterparts could not do it, and the Europeans (White Anglo-Saxon Protestants) could not do it. The climate in which Black and Brown people came from, along with the melanin gene—which I believe is a gift from God—allowed them to do things as slaves, which confused their White slave masters.

Now, we are in the twenty-first century and are still fighting for civil rights and civil unrest, and we have the pandemic. People of all color are dealing with the COVID-19 variance outbreak, and over in Afghanistan, the is another social   , with America in the middle of it all. God knows and sees all things. The peace that man is looking for may not come as he may think. God is still in control. The vaccination and the government are trying to control the population of certain people of color. The ride into space and searching for more space because there may not be enough room here on Earth.

Here in America, we have chaotic fires, floods, and protests and even an attack on the capital by a mad man who did not want to leave office peacefully. The prison is not only a building, but it is a prison of the mindset of our country. The control in the population and how people should be represented by race, creed, and neighborhoods is what voting in America has come to. The United States is definitely divided when it comes to civil unrest, social injustice, voting rights, dealing with the variance outbreak, and the type of vaccine one should receive. I hope and pray that this society will soon open up its eyes and realize that we are living in a ball of confusion. Lord, Lord, I need you to help me! When will we come together?

ABOUT THE AUTHOR

The author, Marion L. Reed Sr., wrote this book when he was away from drug addiction. He had real-life experiences with drugs and with people, places, and things. God inspired him to complete his assignment—and this book is his assignment. He is a man of God! He was also inspired by his uncle, James Warren Reed Jr.

www.ingramcontent.com/pod-product-compliance
Lightning Source LLC
Chambersburg PA
CBHW061719120626
46550CB00003B/1293